World-Changing SCIENTISTS

Marie Curie

Alix Wood

PowerKiDS press.

New York

Published in 2019 by Rosen Publishing
29 East 21st Street, New York, NY 10010

Cataloging-in-Publication Data

Names: Wood, Alix.
Title: Marie Curie / Alix Wood.
Description: New York : PowerKids Press, 2019. | Series: World-changing scientists |
Includes glossary and index.
Identifiers: LCCN ISBN 9781538337813 (pbk.) | ISBN 9781538337820 (library bound)
| ISBN 9781538337837 (6 pack)
Subjects: LCSH: Curie, Marie, 1867-1934--Juvenile literature. | Women physicists-
-Poland--Biography--Juvenile literature. | Women physicists--France--Biography-
-Juvenile literature. | Physicists--Poland--Biography--Juvenile literature. |
Physicists--France--Biography--Juvenile literature. | Women chemists--Poland--
Biography--Juvenile literature. | Women chemists--France--Biography--Juvenile
literature. | Chemists--Poland--Biography--Juvenile literature. | Chemists--France--
Biography--Juvenile literature.
Classification: LCC QD22.C8 W64 2019 | DDC 540.92 B--dc23

Adaptations to North American edition © 2019
by Rosen Publishing

Produced for Rosen Publishing by Alix Wood Books
Designed by Alix Wood
Editor: Eloise Macgregor

Photo credits:
Cover, 1, 4, 8 top, 11 bottom, 12, 19, 25, 26 © Adobe Stock Images; 5, 27 © Alix Wood;
6 © Dennis G. Jarvis; 10 © United States Library of Congress; 14 © Jędrzej Pełka; 16 ©
Royal Institution; 17 © Paul Nadar; 21
© pexels.com; 23 © Polish National Digital Archive/ Narodowe Archiwum Cyfrowe; 24 © Wellcome
images; all other images are in the public domain

Printed in the United States of America

CPSIA compliance information: Batch #CS18PK: For further information contact Rosen Publishing, New York,
New York at 1-800-542-2595.

Contents

World -Changing Scientist

Marie Curie

Marie Skłodowska Curie was a Polish physicist and chemist. Curie is famous for her groundbreaking research on **radioactivity**. She also discovered two new **chemical elements**. Curie was working at a time in history when few women were scientists. In her home country of Poland, women were not even allowed to study at university. Curie was the first woman to win a **Nobel Prize**. She was the first person, and only woman, to have won the prize twice. Curie is also the only person to have won the Nobel Prize in two different sciences, physics and chemistry.

Marie Curie was the first woman professor at the University of Paris.

What Is the Nobel Prize?

Swedish inventor and businessman Alfred Nobel left an enormous fortune in his will. He asked for it to be used to award prizes to people who had benefited mankind in the fields of physics, chemistry, medicine, literature, and peace. Winners of the prize receive a diploma, a medal, and 10 million Swedish crowns. It is a great honor to win a Nobel Prize.

Science Notes

What Is Radioactivity?

Every element in the Universe is made out of tiny **atoms**. Inside each atom is a center known as the **nucleus**. Inside the nucleus there are tiny **protons** and **neutrons**. Very stable elements have the same number of protons and neutrons. Unstable elements are unstable because their nucleus has either too many protons or too many neutrons. This imbalance makes atoms decay, and give off nuclear radiation. Elements that do this are described as being "radioactive."

an atom

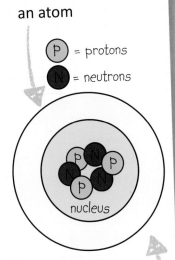

P = protons

N = neutrons

nucleus

This element is very stable, as its atoms have the same number of protons and neutrons.

"Nothing in life is to be feared, it is only to be understood. Now is the time to understand more, so that we may fear less."

MARIE CURIE

A Childhood in Poland

Marie Curie, born Maria Sklodowska, was born in Warsaw, Poland, in 1867. Her mother, Bronislawa, and father, Wladyslaw, were teachers. Curie was the youngest of five children.

Education was very important to Curie's family. Her father taught math and physics, and was the director of two schools for boys. Her mother ran a **boarding school** for girls. It was a difficult time to be a teacher in Poland. Warsaw was ruled by Russia at that time, and there were strict rules about what could be taught in school.

A Divided Poland

In 1772, Russia, Prussia (present-day Germany), and Austria took over and divided Poland between them. Many Poles fought to get back their independence. The Curies lived in the part of Poland that was ruled by Russia. To try to stop a Polish rebellion, the Russians had banned reading and writing in the Polish language. Even more importantly for Curie, students in Polish schools were not allowed to learn how to do laboratory work.

Marie Curie was born in the house on the right-hand side of this street in Warsaw.

Maria, her father Wladyslaw, and her sisters Bronislawa (known as Bronya) and Helena.

Curie's father, Wladyslaw, was a big influence on her childhood. He encouraged her interest in math and science. He also loved books and wrote poetry. The family would gather around the table in the evenings and read Polish poems and stories together.

Wladyslaw was eventually fired from his teaching job by his Russian supervisors because of his anti-Russian views. He had to take lower-paid jobs, and the family had to take in schoolboy lodgers to help pay the bills.

Tragedy struck the Curie family when Marie was seven years old. Her eldest sister, Zofia, died, and then three years later, her mother also died. Without a mother to care for her, Marie was sent to a boarding school.

Marie later went to a selective school. Only the smartest children could attend. At age 15, Marie graduated and won the gold medal, awarded to the top student of that year.

Marie's education then came up against two big problems. Her father did not have enough money to send her away to university, and higher education was not available for girls in Poland. Marie's sister Bronya faced exactly the same problems.

The girls came up with a plan. Marie agreed to work as a tutor and **governess** to pay for Bronya to study medicine in Paris, France. Then, Bronya would pay for Marie to go to university, once she had finished her own studies.

While Curie worked as a governess, she also taught many other local children, who she felt were not getting a proper education.

Marie Curie, aged 16.

> "We taught the smaller children as well as older girls, who wanted to learn to read and write. We also shared Polish books, which the parents appreciated as well. Even this innocent bit of education was dangerous, because all such initiatives were banned by the government and could mean jail time or deportation to Siberia."
>
> MARIE CURIE

Most evenings after work, Marie read chemistry, physics, and math textbooks. She went to classes at an illegal, secret university that Polish rebels had set up. The university taught Polish culture and practical science, and accepted woman students. To avoid **detection**, the classes often changed location, moving from private home to private home, so it became known as the Flying (or Floating) University.

Marie finally got to experiment in a science laboratory, secretly run by her uncle. She had enjoyed her first experiments, and decided that she wanted to study math and physics in Paris.

While Marie was working as a governess for relatives of her father, she fell in love with their son, Kazimierz Zorawski. His parents would not allow their son to marry a penniless relative. He later went on to become a well-respected mathematician at the university in Warsaw.

Moving to Paris

In 1890, Bronya had finished her studies. She invited Marie to join her in Paris. Marie had to refuse the offer, as she had not managed to save enough money. It took her another year and a half before she had enough to pay for her university tuition. In 1891, when Marie was 24, she left Warsaw for Paris. She studied hard. In the evenings, she worked as a tutor to earn her keep. Curie got her degree in physics, coming second out of her whole class. She then got a math degree, and graduated first in her class!

Soon after, she met her future husband, Pierre Curie. He asked her to marry him, but Marie was not sure. She was worried that marrying a Frenchman would mean that she would never go back to her beloved Poland. She returned to Warsaw to look for work, but was instead offered a job at a laboratory at the Sorbonne, a famous university in Paris. She moved back to France, and in July 1895 she married Pierre.

Paris in 1890

Pierre and Marie Curie, photographed around 1895.

Marie and Pierre's love of science had brought them together. Pierre was a teacher at the School of Physics and Chemistry. They were introduced to each other by a Polish physics professor who thought Pierre may be able to offer Marie some laboratory space for her experiments. Pierre found room in the corner of his lab where Marie could work.

Science Notes

Marie Curie's first paid laboratory job was to study different kinds of steel to find out which made the best magnets. Carbon steel magnets were considered the strongest magnets until around 1880. Curie discovered adding tungsten, chromium, or molybdenum produced even better magnets. Many factories began to use tungsten.

Marie encouraged Pierre to complete his studies and become a professor. Pierre was already a respected industrial scientist and inventor. When he was only 21 years old, Pierre and his brother Jacques discovered **piezoelectricity**. Their work needed really accurate measurements, so Pierre also invented an instrument they could use, now known as the Curie scale.

Science Notes

Piezoelectricity

"Piezo" is Greek for "push". Pierre Curie discovered that if you squeeze certain **crystals**, such as quartz, you can make electricity flow through them. This technology is used today, helping quartz watches to keep regular time.

Normally, a crystal's electrical charges are perfectly balanced – a **positive charge** in one place cancels out a nearby **negative charge**. If you squeeze or stretch a piezoelectric crystal, you push atoms closer together or further apart. This upsets the balance of positive and negative, and causes electrical charges.

Pierre and Magnetism

Like Marie, Pierre also studied magnetism. Pierre discovered that a change of temperature affected how magnetic something was. Now known as the Curie temperature, or Curie point, Pierre measured and recorded the different temperatures at which certain materials lost their magnetic properties.

Marie and her two daughters, Ève and Irène.

In 1896, Henri Becquerel discovered that **uranium** salts gave off rays that resembled **X-rays**. Marie decided to study uranium rays. She used the device that Pierre had invented for measuring electric charge. With it, she discovered that air around uranium rays conducted electricity. The more uranium she added, the more reaction Marie got. Marie realized that the radiation wasn't coming from other substances interacting with uranium; it was coming from the uranium itself!

At about this time, Marie and Pierre's daughter Irène was born. Curie had to go back to teaching to support her family.

An Exciting Discovery

Marie taught all day and did her research in her spare time. She experimented with different **minerals** containing uranium. Marie found that two of them, pitchblende and torbernite, gave off radiation, too. In fact, pitchblende was four times more active than uranium itself, and torbernite was twice as active. She realized these two minerals must contain small quantities of another substance that was far more radioactive than uranium!

pitchblende

Pierre stopped his own research on crystals and started to help Marie study pitchblende. They discovered a completely new, radioactive element. They named it polonium, in honor of Marie's homeland. A few months later, the Curies discovered a second element, which they named radium, the Latin word for "ray."

Extracting the radium and polonium from the pitchblende was hard work. Curie had to refine many tons of the ore to get the tiniest amounts.

"Sometimes I had to spend a whole day mixing a boiling mass with a heavy iron rod nearly as large as myself. I would be broken with fatigue at the day's end."

MARIE CURIE

Science Notes

Dangerous Radiation

Marie and Pierre did not realize how much danger they were putting themselves in while studying radioactive elements. The Curies' laboratory was a converted shed next to the School of Physics and Chemistry. The shed was poorly ventilated and it leaked. Being exposed to radiation in such an enclosed space was very dangerous. Polonium is around 250,000 times more toxic than deadly hydrogen cyanide. Its radioactivity makes it difficult to handle safely. Polonium can harm people if even the tiniest particles are breathed in, swallowed, or absorbed by the skin. Modern scientists wear special protective clothing when handling polonium.

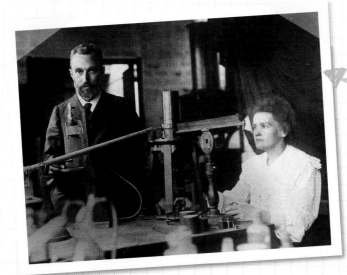

Pierre and Marie Curie in their laboratory.

Fame and Prizes

Between 1898 and 1902, the Curies published several science papers about their work. Marie and Pierre knew they needed to announce their discoveries before someone else beat them to it. The couple became celebrities in the world of science.

In 1903, Marie was awarded a doctorate from the University of Paris for her work titled "Researches on Radioactive Substances." Shortly afterward, the couple were invited to the Royal Institution in London to give a speech on radioactivity. However, Marie was not allowed to speak, because she was a woman!

This 1904 painting by Henry Jamyn Brooks shows women in the audience at a Royal Institution lecture, but women were not allowed to give a talk!

Using Publicity for Good

By naming her new element "polonium," Marie used her publicity to bring the world's attention to Poland's fight for independence. Poland did not officially exist at the time. Curie later said that she wished she had waited, and named radium "polonium" instead. Polonium has fewer uses than radium, so naming radium "polonium" would have brought more worldwide attention to the cause of Poland.

Science Notes

It was difficult for a woman to be taken seriously as a scientist in 1903. When the Curies, together with Henri Becquerel, were considered for the Nobel Prize in Physics for their work, the committee objected to including a woman. Pierre had to insist that the original research was Marie's, so she, too, would rightly be awarded the prize.

Henri Bequerel

Henri Becquerel was a French physicist, and the first person to discover evidence of radioactivity. His work inspired Marie to study uranium. The unit for measuring radioactivity, the becquerel (Bq), is named after him.

A Dreadful Accident

On April 19, 1906, Pierre Curie went to meet some colleagues for lunch. When he left, he was running late for a meeting. It was raining heavily. As Pierre crossed the busy Rue Dauphine, he was struck by a horse-drawn vehicle. He slipped and fell under its wheels, which fractured his skull. He died instantly.

The police waited at the family home until Marie came back from a day out with her daughter Irène. Newspaper reporters said that when Marie was told of Pierre's death she took the news calmly. It was only when Pierre's brother Jacques arrived to comfort her that Marie was able to cry.

A magazine illustration of Pierre's accident.

Front Page News?

Pierre Curie's death was a major international news story the day after the accident, but it was not the day's headline. A devastating earthquake had happened in San Francisco the same day. Nevertheless, his death was the front page news in most French papers.

> "Crushed by the blow, I did not feel able to face the future. I could not forget, however, what my husband used to say, that even deprived of him, I ought to continue my work."
>
> MARIE CURIE

Encouraged by Jacques, Marie returned to her work. The French government offered to support her and the children with a state pension. Marie firmly refused the offer, saying that she was quite capable of supporting her family herself.

Marie received another unexpected offer. Pierre had recently been appointed professor of physics at Sorbonne University. Marie worked as superintendent of his laboratory. After Pierre's death, the university invited her to take his place as professor. She accepted, and became the first woman professor at the University of Paris.

Helping the War Effort

The First World War began in 1914. German troops invaded France and headed toward Paris. Marie did not want her precious radium falling into enemy hands. She put it in a lead-lined container, and took it by train to Bordeaux, many miles south of Paris. She placed the container in a safety deposit box at a Bordeaux bank, and returned to Paris.

Without her radium, she was unable to continue her work. She decided to use her science skills to help fight the war, instead. Marie invented a mobile X-ray unit to treat wounded soldiers at the battlefields. The Union of Women of France gave her enough money to produce one vehicle. Known as a Little Curie, the vehicle was so useful treating the wounded at the Battle of Marne that more cars were needed. Marie asked her wealthy friends to donate vehicles. Soon she had 20 Little Curies. She trained 150 women volunteers to operate them, including her daughter Irène.

Marie operated her own Little Curie at the front.

Curie also oversaw the building of 200 X-ray rooms at the field hospitals behind the battle lines. Because of her efforts, around one million wounded soldiers received X-ray exams during the war!

> "The use of the X-rays during the war saved the lives of many wounded men; it also saved many from long suffering and lasting infirmity."
>
> MARIE CURIE

Science Notes

How Do X-Rays Work?

X-ray technology was invented by accident in 1895. German physicist Wilhelm Roentgen was experimenting with **electron beams**. He noticed that a covered **fluorescent** screen in his lab glowed when the electron beam was turned on. Roentgen put his hand in front of the screen, and saw his bones appear! Soft tissue, such as skin, is made up of small atoms. They do not absorb X-rays very well. The **calcium** atoms in bones are much larger, so they absorb X-rays. X-rays let doctors see through human tissue and help find broken bones or swallowed objects easily.

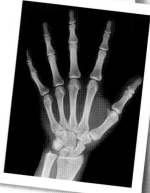

American Generosity

After Marie and Pierre had won the Nobel Prize in 1903, the University of Paris and the Pasteur Institute decided to build a Radium Institute. The Curie laboratory, headed by Marie, would look at the physics and chemistry of radium. The Pasteur laboratory studied the biology and medical applications of radioactivity. Curie's laboratory was completed in August 1914. Marie dedicated most of the rest of her life to the Institute. She considered it a tribute to Pierre's memory, and a way to help society.

To raise funds for the Paris Institute, Marie agreed to be interviewed by Mrs. William Brown Meloney, the editor of an American women's magazine. Curie talked about how she needed more radium for her research. She joked that the U.S. had around 50 times as much radium as she, the scientist who had discovered the element, had! Meloney organized a campaign to get her another gram of radium. In spring 1921, Curie and her daughters traveled to the U.S. to meet the President.

From left to right – Mrs. Meloney, Irène, Marie, and Ève Curie in the U.S.

President Warren G. Harding presented Marie with a gram of radium, bought with funds raised by American women. At the presentation, Marie wore the same black dress she had worn to both Nobel ceremonies. Curie was not interested in clothes and fashion.

> "I have no dress except the one I wear every day. If you are going to be kind enough to give me one, please let it be practical and dark so that I can put it on afterwards to go to the laboratory."
>
> MARIE CURIE

A Radium Institute for Warsaw

Marie's sister, Bronya, supervised fundraising in Poland to open a Radium Institute in Warsaw, too. She sold bricks featuring Marie's image to raise funds. On Marie's second trip to the U.S. she met with President Herbert Hoover. He presented her with money to help equip her Warsaw Institute, too.

Her Death and Her Legacy

On July 4, 1934, Marie Curie died in hospital in Passy, France, from a disease of the blood. It is now believed her illness was caused by her work. The damaging effects of radiation were not known at the time, so Marie did not use the safety measures that scientists would today. She sometimes put radioactive material in her pocket or kept it in her desk, noticing how the test tubes lit up at night! Curie's war work also repeatedly exposed her to harmful X-rays.

As we now know how dangerous radioactivity can be, Curie's notes are thought to be too dangerous for people to touch! Her papers are kept in lead-lined boxes, and anyone reading them must wear protective clothing.

Marie Curie's radioactive notebook.

"One of our joys was to go into our workroom at night ... It was really a lovely sight and one always new to us. The glowing tubes looked like faint, fairy lights."

MARIE CURIE

Irène working in the laboratory with her mother, Marie.

A Family Legacy

The Curie's legacy lived on through their children. Marie's daughter Irène Joliot-Curie was awarded the Nobel Prize in Chemistry in 1935 with her husband, Frédéric. Irène and Frédéric's children, Hélène and Pierre, are also well-known scientists. Marie's younger daughter, Ève, wrote a biography about her famous mother, which was turned into a feature film.

In 1995, Marie and Pierre Curie's remains were moved from their burial place and placed in the Panthéon in Paris, the final resting place of France's greatest minds. Marie became the first woman to be buried there on her own merits.

A Warsaw statue of Marie Curie holding an atom of polonium by Bronislaw Krzysztof.

Science Project

Experiments with Magnets

Marie and Pierre Curie experimented with magnetism early in their careers. Marie investigated what materials made the best magnets. Pierre studied how magnets were affected by changes of temperature. He noticed that magnetic material lost its magnetism when heated to a certain temperature. Based on his research, he came up with a scale, known as the Curie scale. It has been used by scientists ever since. The Curie scale records at what temperature each different material loses its magnetism.

There are two good reasons not to try a magnet-heating experiment at home. One reason is that you would have to use boiling hot water to heat your magnet, and that would be dangerous if the water splashed on you. The other really good reason is that afterward, your magnet wouldn't work anymore! In this experiment, you will look at what happens to a magnet if you lower its temperature. Can you predict what might happen?

Try this experiment to see how a magnet is affected by freezing temperatures.

You Will Need:

- a magnet
- metal paper clips
- plastic tongs
- a bowl of ice water
- gloves
- a nonmetallic bowl
- a freezer
- a thermometer

1

First, test how strong your magnet is at room temperature. Fill the bowl with paper clips. Put the magnet in the bowl, lift it out, and record how many paper clips stuck to the magnet. Then replace the paper clips into the bowl.

2

Place a bowl of ice water into the freezer until it reaches 32 degrees F (0 degrees C). Place the magnet in the bowl and put it in the freezer for 15 minutes.

3

Take the bowl out of the freezer. Using the tongs, remove the magnet from the water and place it in the bowl of paper clips.

4

Record how many paper clips the magnet picked up. Was it more or less than the room temperature magnet? What conclusion can you make?

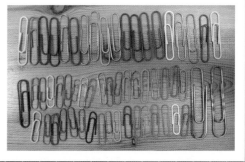

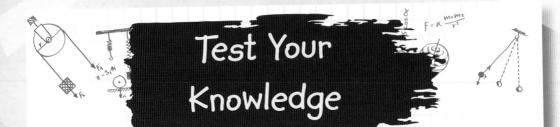

Test Your Knowledge

Test your science knowledge and your memory with this quiz about Marie Curie and her work. Can you get them all right? Answers are at the bottom of page 29.

1 Marie Curie is well-known for discovering what?
a) digital radio   b) radioactivity   c) radio waves

2 What is the center of an atom known as?
a) the nucleus   b) the middleus   c) the centreus

3 Why didn't Poland officially exist when Curie lived there?
a) It is a new country
b) Someone had forgotten to draw it on a map
c) Russia, Prussia, and Austria had divided it between them

4 What was Poland's Flying University?
a) A school that taught people how to fly
b) A secret university that kept moving to avoid discovery
c) A very quick way of studying

5 Pierre Curie invented piezoelectricity. What modern instrument uses piezoelectricity to keep time?
a) a television   b) a drum   c) a quartz watch

6 Why did Curie and her sister go to Paris to study?
a) Polish universities did not accept women
b) They liked France
c) They spoke French

7 Marie Curie discovered two chemical elements. What were they?
a) polonium and radium
b) radium and plutonium
c) polonium and plutonium

8 Why do modern scientists wear protective clothing when handling radioactive elements such as radium?
a) Scientists like wearing special clothing
b) It helps keep the material clean
c) Radioactive material is very dangerous

9 What was a "Little Curie"?
a) an X-ray   b) a mobile X-ray vehicle   c) Marie's daughter

10 What did President Warren G. Harding present Curie with?
a) a gram of radium   b) a dress   c) a prize

Answers

1. b – radioactivity; 2. a – the nucleus; 3. c – Russia, Prussia, and Austria had divided it between them; 4. b – A secret university that kept moving to avoid discovery; 5. c – a quartz watch; 6. a – Polish universities did not accept women; 7. a – polonium and radium; 8. c – Radioactive material is very dangerous; 9. b – a mobile X-ray vehicle; 10. a – a gram of radium

Glossary

atoms The smallest particles of an element.

boarding school A school at which most pupils live during the term.

calcium A silver-white soft metallic element that helps make up the bodies of most plants and animals.

chemical elements Substances that cannot be chemically broken down into simpler substances.

crystals Solid forms of a substance or mixture that have regularly repeating internal arrangements of their atoms.

detection The act of being discovered.

electron beams A group of nearly parallel lines of electromagnetic radiation.

fluorescent Giving off radiation usually as light when exposed to radiation from another source.

governess A woman who teaches a child in a private home.

minerals Solid chemical elements or compounds that occur naturally in the form of crystals and are not from living or once-living matter.

negative charge A charge that has more electrons than protons.

neutrons Uncharged atomic particles present in all known atomic nuclei except hydrogens.

Nobel Prize An annual prize established by the will of Alfred Nobel awarded to people who work for the interests of humanity.

nucleus The central part of an atom that consists of protons and usually neutrons.

piezoelectricity Electricity due to pressure especially in a crystalline substance.

positive charge A charge that has less electrons than protons.

protons An atomic particle in the nucleus of every atom that carries a positive charge.

radioactivity The giving off of rays of energy or particles by the breaking apart of atoms of certain elements.

uranium A silvery heavy radioactive metallic element.

X-rays Images of the internal composition of something.

For More Information

Bolt Simons, Lisa M. *Marie Curie: Physicist and Chemist* (STEM Scientists and Inventors). Mankato, MN: Capstone Press, 2018.

O'Quinn, Amy M. *Marie Curie for Kids: Her Life and Scientific Discoveries, with 21 Activities and Experiments* (For Kids series). Chicago, IL: Chicago Review Press, 2016.

Rowell, Rebecca. *Marie Curie Advances the Study of Radioactivity* (Great Moments in Science). Minneapolis, MN: Core Library, 2016.

Stine, Megan. *Who Was Marie Curie?* New York, NY: Penguin Workshop, 2014.

Websites
Due to the changing nature of Internet links, PowerKids Press has developed an online list of websites related to the subject of this book. This site is updated regularly. Please use this link to access the list:

www.powerkidslinks.com/wcs/curie

Index